ISAAC ASIMOV'S
Library of the Universe

PLUTO:
A Double Planet?

by Isaac Asimov

Gareth Stevens Publishing
Milwaukee

Library of Congress Cataloging-in-Publication Data

Asimov, Isaac, 1920-
   Pluto: a double planet.

   (Isaac Asimov's library of the universe)
   Bibliography: p.
   Includes index.
   Summary: Introduces this small, distant, and mysterious planet, surveying its
discovery sixty years ago, peculiar orbit, and recently discovered satellite.
   1. Pluto (Planet)—Juvenile literature. [1. Pluto (Planet)] I. Title. II. Series:
Asimov, Isaac, 1920-   Library of the universe.
QB701.A85   1989   /523.4'82   89-11290
ISBN 1-55532-373-1

A Gareth Stevens Children's Books edition
Edited, designed, and produced by
Gareth Stevens, Inc.
RiverCenter Building, Suite 201
1555 North RiverCenter Drive
Milwaukee, Wisconsin 53212, USA

**For a free color catalog describing Gareth Stevens' list of high-quality children's
books call 1-800-341-3569.**

Cover painting © Paul Dimare

Project editor: Mark Sachner
Series design: Laurie Shock
Book design: Kate Kriege
Research editor: Kathleen Weisfeld Barrilleaux
Picture research: Matthew Groshek
Technical advisers and consulting editors: Julian Baum and Francis Reddy

Printed in the United States of America

1 2 3 4 5 6 7 8 9 95 94 93 92 91 90

CONTENTS

Nowadays, we have seen planets up close, all the way to distant Uranus and Neptune. We have mapped Venus through its clouds. We have seen dead volcanoes on Mars and live ones on Io, one of Jupiter's satellites. We have detected strange objects no one knew anything about till recently: quasars, pulsars, black holes. We have studied stars not only by the light they give out, but by other kinds of radiation: infrared, ultraviolet, x-rays, radio waves. We have even detected tiny particles called neutrinos that are given off by the stars.

The most distant, the smallest, and the most mysterious known planet in our Solar system is Pluto, which was discovered only recently, in 1930. In this book, let's consider Pluto, how it was discovered, its peculiar orbit, and its satellite, Charon — which was discovered only a few years ago.

Isaac Asimov

A Planet Waiting to Be Discovered

You might be surprised at how much we keep on learning about our Solar system.

As recently as the 1920s, the two farthest known planets were Uranus and Neptune. There were some things about Uranus and Neptune that astronomers could figure out, such as their orbits around the Sun.

But even when astronomers considered the gravitational pull of every known planet, they could not completely explain the motions of Uranus and Neptune. Tiny errors remained. Could there be an undiscovered planet farther out that <u>also</u> pulled on Uranus and Neptune?

Astronomers watched the sky to see if they could find a new, far-away planet.

Opposite: Like dancers in a celestial ballet, the planets circle our Sun, held in orbit by its gravitational pull. The gravity of each planet also adds a tiny pull to every other planet.

Below: an orrery (OR-reh-ree), a mechanical model of the Solar system — without Pluto and Neptune, the two most recently discovered planets.

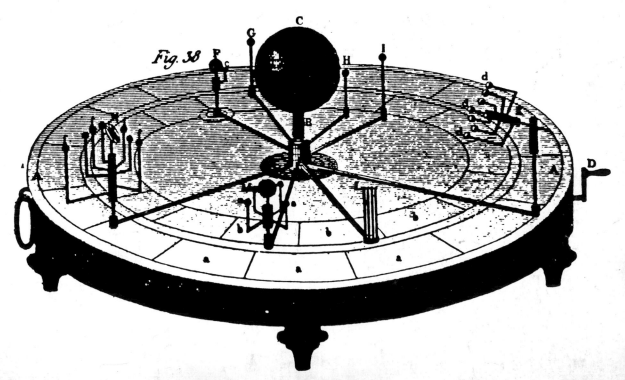

P

Name that planet!

Most of the bodies in the Solar system are named for characters in Greek and Roman myths. When Pluto was discovered, an 11-year-old English schoolgirl, Venetia Burney, suggested that the new planet was so far from the Sun it must get only dim light — so it should be named for Pluto, the god of the underworld. That was accepted. As an added bonus, the first two letters, PL, memorialize Percival Lowell, who built the observatory where Pluto was detected.

The Discovery of Pluto

In Arizona in 1894, an astronomer, Percival Lowell, built an observatory known as the Lowell Observatory. There he searched for the new planet. He calculated where it ought to be to pull at Uranus and Neptune properly, but he died in 1916 without finding it.

Astronomer Clyde Tombaugh found Pluto in 1930 after viewing hundreds of photographs.

A young man named Clyde Tombaugh picked up Lowell's mission at the observatory. Tombaugh took photographs of particular parts of the sky on different days. He used a device that showed first one photo and then the other in rapid succession. The stars didn't move, but a planet would.

On February 18, 1930, Tombaugh came up with a pair of photographs in which one dot moved. It was an exciting discovery. The "moving dot" was a new planet. Its name: Pluto.

Opposite: Pluto, Greek and Roman god of the underworld.

Below: the first photos of Pluto. These pictures, taken one week apart, show that one "star" has moved — the planet Pluto.

The Long Orbit

As the farthest known planet, Pluto is nearly 3.7 billion miles (5.9 billion km) from the Sun, on the average. This is about 40 times as far from the Sun as Earth is. This means that Pluto has to travel along an orbit 40 times as long as Earth's to make one complete circle around the Sun.

At Pluto's great distance, the Sun's gravity is so weak that Pluto travels only one-sixth as fast around the Sun as Earth does. And because of its long orbit and slow motion, Pluto takes 248 Earth years to make <u>one</u> <u>circle</u> around the Sun!

Not until the year <u>2178</u> will Pluto finally be back at the place in the sky where it was discovered in 1930.

Opposite: Recent research shows that Pluto is more than a distant ice ball. Most of it is made of rock, with a thick coating of ice. The thin top layer is made of frozen methane.

Below: Pluto travels a longer path around the Sun, but it also moves more slowly than any planet. The shaded areas show that since 1930, Neptune has moved one-third of its way around the Sun (inner orbit), and Pluto less than one-fourth (outer orbit).

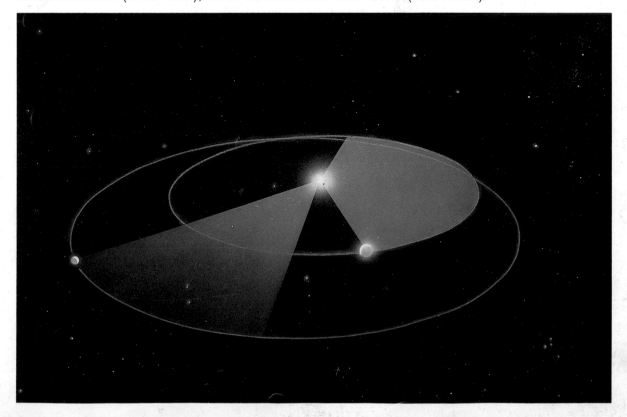

The origins of Pluto —
a cosmic escapee?

Could Pluto once have been a
satellite? It's no bigger than a middle-
sized moon, and thanks to its
lopsided orbit it moves in closer to
the Sun than Neptune. So some
astronomers think it might once have
been a satellite of Neptune that got
knocked away in some cosmic
catastrophe. They have traced its
orbit back in time, but it doesn't
seem that it was ever close
enough to Neptune to have been
its satellite. So how was it
formed? We really don't know.

Pluto's Trespassing Orbit

The planets do not travel about the Sun in circles, but in slightly lopsided, or egg-shaped, orbits called ellipses. A planet in an elliptical orbit is a little closer to the Sun at one end of its orbit than at the other.

Pluto's orbit is <u>quite</u> lopsided. At its farthest it is about 4.6 billion miles (7.4 billion km) from the Sun, but at its closest it is only 2.75 billion miles (4.4 billion km) from the Sun. This is actually a little closer to the Sun than Neptune is.

Does that mean the planets might collide? No. Pluto's orbit is tilted, so it moves under Neptune's orbit and the two planets never come closer than 235 million miles (378 million km) to each other.

Opposite: Is Pluto an escaped moon of Neptune? It's an interesting thought, but most astronomers doubt it. Small as it is, Pluto seems to be a world in its own right.

Below: Pluto's orbit takes the planet far from the plane in which the other planets orbit. At its closest to the Sun, Pluto is actually closer than Neptune!

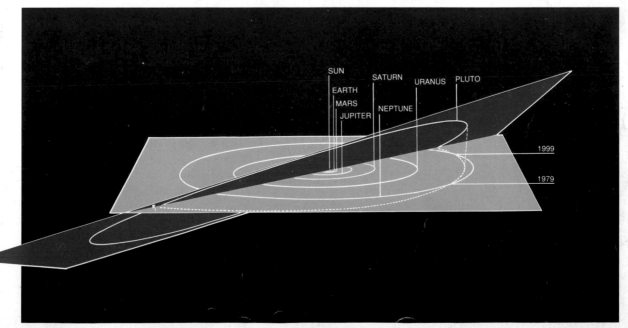

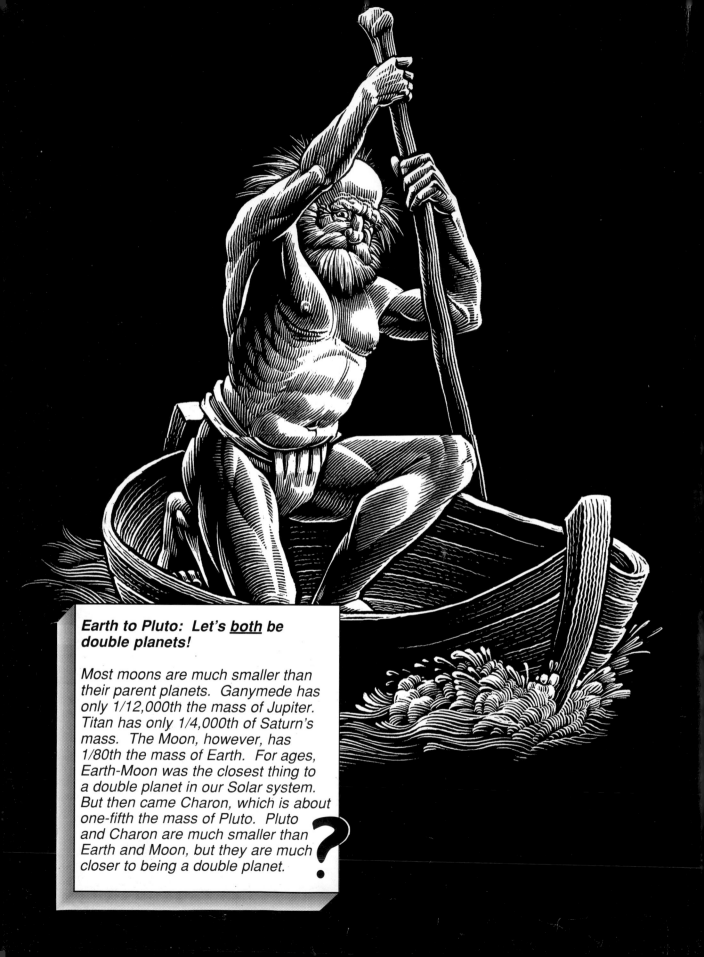

Earth to Pluto: Let's <u>both</u> be double planets!

Most moons are much smaller than their parent planets. Ganymede has only 1/12,000th the mass of Jupiter. Titan has only 1/4,000th of Saturn's mass. The Moon, however, has 1/80th the mass of Earth. For ages, Earth-Moon was the closest thing to a double planet in our Solar system. But then came Charon, which is about one-fifth the mass of Pluto. Pluto and Charon are much smaller than Earth and Moon, but they are much closer to being a double planet.

Charon — Pluto's Partner

Between 1979 and 1999, Pluto is closer to the Sun than Neptune is, and it can be seen better than at any other time. On June 22, 1978, astronomer James W. Christy noticed a bulge on a photograph he had taken of Pluto. He looked at earlier photos and found the bulge in different spots.

Christy showed that Pluto had a satellite moving about it. According to Christy, he named the moon Charon (pronounced Sharon) with his wife Char in mind. But by a stroke of good luck, Charon had another identity: Charon (pronounced KAIR-on) the boatman from Greek mythology who transported spirits to the underworld — the realm of the god Pluto.

Charon is about half as wide as Pluto is. No other known planet has a satellite that close to being as large as itself. This means that Pluto is practically a double planet. Only Earth and its Moon, which is about one-quarter the width of Earth, come that close to being a double planet.

Opposite: Charon, boatman of the Greek underworld.

Above: an artist's concept of Pluto and Charon in the early days, forming from the rocky debris at the edge of the Solar system. This is one idea of how Charon formed.

Below: This picture may not reveal much to you, but to astronomer James Christy it showed that Pluto had a moon. The bulge (right) appeared in different places in other pictures.

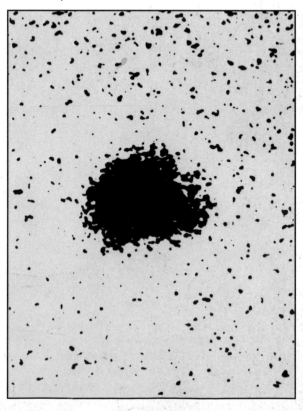

Too Small to See

When astronomers searched for Pluto they thought it would be fairly large, so it would pull sufficiently at Neptune and Uranus. But Pluto was much dimmer than they had expected. And as they studied it, it proved to be much smaller than they had expected, too.

On June 9, 1988, Pluto moved in front of a star. Based on the time that the star remained hidden, astronomers could calculate that Pluto was 1,457 miles (2,344 km) across — smaller than our Moon. In fact, Pluto weighs only about one-fifth as much as our Moon, and Charon weighs only one-fifth as much as Pluto. They are very small worlds indeed. And considering how far away from us they are, it is hard to see anything on them.

When Pluto passed between Earth and a bright star, astronomers got the chance to search for a thin atmosphere around the planet. As Pluto eclipsed the bright star, sensitive instruments searched the star's light for any changes caused by gases surrounding Pluto. Astronomers aboard NASA's Kuiper Airborne Observatory (inset), a telescope-equipped jet plane, were the first to detect Pluto's thin atmosphere.

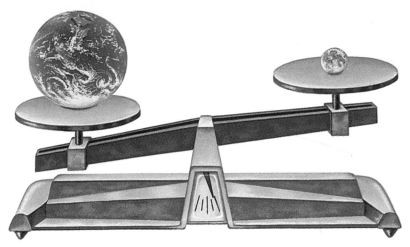

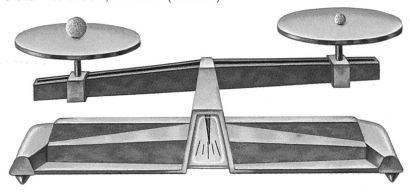

Earth is 80 times more massive than the Moon (top scales), but Pluto is just eight times more massive than its moon, Charon (bottom).

Below: Charon may have formed from the cloud of debris created when an asteroid or comet collided with Pluto long ago.

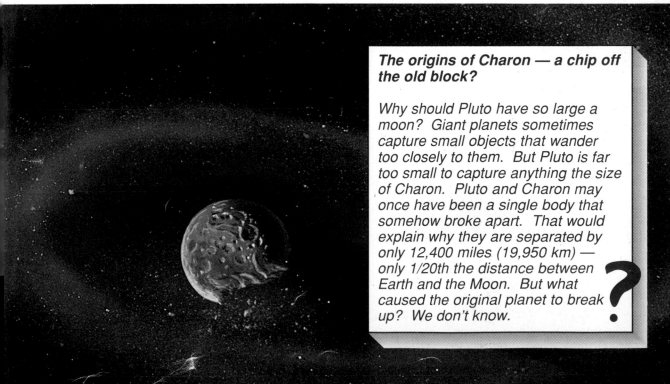

The origins of Charon — a chip off the old block?

Why should Pluto have so large a moon? Giant planets sometimes capture small objects that wander too closely to them. But Pluto is far too small to capture anything the size of Charon. Pluto and Charon may once have been a single body that somehow broke apart. That would explain why they are separated by only 12,400 miles (19,950 km) — only 1/20th the distance between Earth and the Moon. But what caused the original planet to break up? We don't know.

Electronic Pictures

Despite its small size and great distance from Earth, astronomers have managed to make out some details about Pluto.

In the 1950s, they found that Pluto's light grew slightly dimmer and then slightly brighter every 6.4 days. They realized this was because Pluto turned on its axis in that time, showing a brighter side and a dimmer side as it turned.

Then, in 1976, by analyzing light reflected from Pluto, astronomers showed that it was covered with frozen methane, a chemical found in natural gas on Earth. They also found that Pluto is lighter at its poles and darker at its equator.

Opposite: On Earth, pockets of natural gas, which contains methane, accompany oil deep underground. Here, an oil refinery burns off excess methane.

Below: When it's summertime on Pluto, the planet's thin layer of frozen methane turns to a gas and creates an atmosphere. Darker material beneath the ice then becomes visible, and Pluto appears dimmer (left). When winter comes, the gases in the atmosphere freeze and brighten Pluto with a fresh coat of methane snow (right).

The Pluto-Charon Eclipses

When Pluto's orbit brings it nearest to Earth, Charon moves in front of it and then behind it every 6.4 days. Astronomers discovered Charon just in time to study these eclipses.

By studying the light of Pluto when Charon is hidden behind it, and both together when Charon is in front, astronomers have found that Charon is darker than Pluto.

Standing on Charon during one of its rare eclipses of Pluto, you could watch the dark shadow of your world sweep across the frozen surface of Pluto.

Pluto is big enough — and cold enough, from -350°F (-212°C) down to -390°F (-234°C) — to have a thin atmosphere of methane gas. Charon is just as cold, although it is smaller and has less gravity, so it has lost its methane and is made up of water ice.

But Pluto and Charon are so close in distance and in size that particles in Pluto's atmosphere extend to Charon. These form a thin methane cloud over the entire Pluto-Charon system. So Pluto-Charon is a double planet enclosed in a single atmosphere!

Right: When Charon passes in front of Pluto, astronomers call it an "inferior eclipse." When the shadow of Pluto falls on Charon, it's a "superior eclipse."

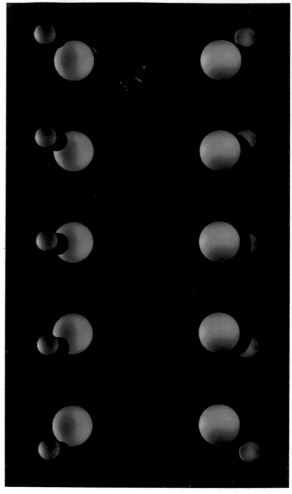

Pluto-Charon —
a cosmic face-off

As a small body circles a larger one its rotation is slowed by tides. This is why a satellite faces only one side to its planet — its speed of rotation has been slowed down. The Moon faces only one side to Earth. The large planet also slows, but it is so massive, it only slows slightly. Only in the case of Pluto and Charon are the two bodies so small and so nearly equal in size that each faces the same side to the other, like two halves of a dumbbell.

Our Starlike Sun — A View from Pluto

Pluto is so far from the Sun that from Pluto's surface, the Sun would look quite different than it does to us here on Earth. If you saw our Sun from Pluto, you might think of it more as a star than you do when you see it in our blue sky on Earth. Even when Pluto is at its closest to the Sun, it gets only about 1/900th as much sunlight as Earth gets. No wonder it's so cold.

Despite its distance, the Sun, even when viewed from remote Pluto, would appear a thousand times brighter than the full Moon as seen from Earth. But because Pluto's thin atmosphere does not scatter sunlight the way ours does on Earth, the stars are visible even when the Sun shines in Pluto's sky.

On Pluto, the Sun appears 14 million times brighter than any other star. After all, even the nearest star is thousands of times as far away from Pluto as the Sun is.

Ice crystals in Pluto's atmosphere create a rare arc of light around the distant Sun. It's the beginning of Pluto's long winter, and methane snow has started to coat the planet's surface as the atmosphere freezes.

Probes to Pluto?

So far, rocket probes have been sent to every other planet in the Solar system. One probe, Voyager 2, even passed near Neptune in August of 1989. But Pluto is not in position right now for Voyager to go anywhere near it. What's more, no Pluto probe is in the works at this time.

Sooner or later, though, it will happen. It may not happen for several generations, but one day a probe will be sent past Jupiter or Saturn in such a way that the gravity of those planets will curve the probe's path and shoot it outward toward Pluto. Then we can get an up-close look at both Pluto and Charon and study their surfaces in detail.

But till then, our best hope for a good look at Pluto-Charon is the Space Telescope. Thanks to its orbit above our planet's atmosphere, it will give us the clearest, least distorted view we have ever had of the cosmos.

Opposite: Perhaps one day next century we'll get our first up-close views of faraway Pluto when space probes fly past the planet.

The Hubble Space Telescope.

Top: A simulated view of a star cluster as seen from Earth. Bottom: The same cluster as "seen" by the Space Telescope.

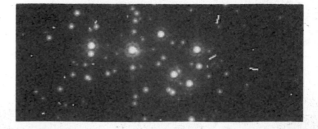

And Now for Planet Number 10

Since Pluto and Charon have turned out to be such small bodies, it seems unlikely that their tiny gravitational pull would be enough to have much of an effect on the orbits of giant Uranus and Neptune. Some astronomers feel that somewhere out there must be Planet X — a tenth planet large enough to affect the outermost planets.

Astronomers study the motions of comets and of probes that move in the outer parts of the Solar system to see if they respond to an unknown gravitational pull. So far, they have found nothing. But it took decades after the discovery of Neptune to detect Pluto, and it may take that long to find Planet X.

Opposite: The Infrared Astronomical Satellite (IRAS), a special telescope sensitive to heat, searched the entire sky for objects too cool to glow by their own light — such as a tenth planet. Inset: An infrared map of the sky. The bright band is the Milky Way.

Below: Astronomer Bob Harrington searches for a planet beyond Pluto. He believes that the clues lay somewhere in the volumes of data returned by IRAS.

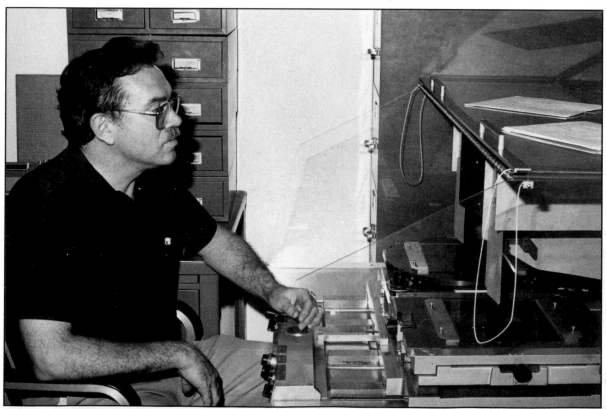

The Solar System's Final Frontier?

Is Pluto — or Planet X — our Solar system's final frontier?

Out beyond Pluto there are smaller bodies, many of them too small to be seen at their great distances. These bodies are distant members of the Solar system "family." Astronomers feel that one such body is now a satellite of Neptune — a captured asteroid that was pushed or pulled into orbit around Neptune. Other smaller bodies, after colliding with each other or being pulled at by distant stars, may approach our Solar system, too.

Comets are such objects. Near the Sun they may vaporize, giving off the dust and gas that produce the comet's tail we see from Earth. Astronomers believe a swarm of many billions of frozen comets called the Oort Cloud circles the Sun far beyond Pluto. Beyond that frontier of the Solar system lie the stars. But who knows what <u>other</u> frontiers of the Solar system lie between us and the stars?

Opposite: In the 22nd century, when Pluto and Charon again eclipse each other, humans may view the events with their own eyes — as interplanetary visitors.

Below: A comet circles far from the Sun in the Oort Cloud.

Fact File: Pluto

Pluto, our Solar system's smallest known planet, is also the farthest from the Sun and takes the longest of any known planet to orbit the Sun — nearly 248 Earth years. Its 1930 discovery also makes it the most recent planet to be detected.

Tiny Pluto is still revealing many of its secrets to astronomers here on Earth. One of Pluto's most exciting secrets — the existence of its moon, Charon — came to light in 1978.

Charon is very close to its "parent" planet in size, mass, and distance. So Pluto and Charon make up the closest thing we know of to a double planet. (Our own Earth and Moon run a respectable but not very close second as a double planet.) And thanks to observations made in 1988, astronomers now feel that Charon and Pluto may even share the same atmosphere!

Three other known planets — Jupiter, Saturn, and Earth — have moons that are bigger than Pluto. In the minds of some astronomers, without its moon and atmosphere, tiny Pluto would barely qualify as a planet at all!

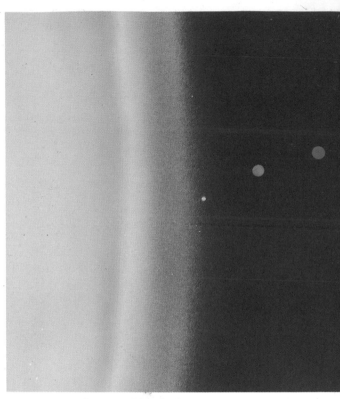

Above: the Sun and its Solar system family, left to right: Mercury, Venus, Earth, Mars, Jupiter, Saturn, Uranus, Neptune, and Pluto.

Pluto's Moon

Name	Diameter	Distance from Pluto's Center
Charon	745 miles (1200 km)	12,700 miles (20,450 km)

Pluto: How It Measures Up to Earth

Planet	Diameter	Rotation Period (length of day)
Pluto	1,457 miles (2,344 km)	6 days, 9 hours, 18 minutes
Earth	7,926 miles (12,756 km)	23 hours, 56 minutes

The Sun and Its Family of Planets

Right: Here is a close-up of Pluto and its moon, Charon. Because Charon is about half as wide as Pluto, many astronomers describe the two as a double planet.

Moons	Period of Orbit Around Sun (length of year)	Surface Gravity	Distance from Sun (nearest-farthest)	Least Time It Takes for Light to Travel to Earth
1	247.7 years	0.06*	2.75-4.58 billion miles (4.43-7.37 billion km)	3.9 hours
1	365.25 days (one year)	1.00*	92-95 million miles (147-152 million km)	—

*Multiply your weight by this number to find out how much you would weigh on this planet.

More Books About Pluto

Here are more books that contain information about Pluto. If you are interested in them, check your library or bookstore.

Discovery of Pluto. Tombaugh (Astronomical Society of the Pacific)
Our Solar System. Asimov (Gareth Stevens)
The Planet Pluto. Whyte (Pergamon)
The Planets. Couper (Franklin Watts)
Whitney's Star Finder. Whitney (Knopf)

Places to Visit

You can explore Pluto and other parts of the Universe without leaving Earth. Here are some museums and centers where you can find many different kinds of space exhibits.

Lowell Observatory
Flagstaff, Arizona

Chamberlin Observatory
Denver, Colorado

Allegheny Observatory
Pittsburgh, Pennsylvania

Griffith Observatory
Los Angeles, California

Memphis Pink Palace Museum and Planetarium
Memphis, Tennessee

Pacific Science Center
Seattle, Washington

Astrocentre — Royal Ontario Museum
Toronto, Ontario

Dow Planetarium
Montreal, Quebec

For More Information About Pluto

Here are some people you can write to for more information about Pluto. Be sure to tell them exactly what you want to know about. And include your full name and address so they can write back to you.

For information about Pluto:
National Space Society
600 Maryland Avenue SW
Washington, DC 20024

The Planetary Society
65 North Catalina
Pasadena, California 91106

Star Date
McDonald Observatory
Austin, Texas 78712

Space Communications Branch
Ministry of State for Science and Technology
240 Sparks Street, C. D. Howe Building
Ottawa, Ontario K1A 1A1, Canada

About planetary missions:
NASA Jet Propulsion Laboratory
4800 Oak Grove Drive
Pasadena, California 91109

NASA Kennedy Space Center
Educational Services Office
Kennedy Space Center, Florida 32899

Alabama Space and Rocket Center
Space Camp Applications
One Tranquility Base
Huntsville, Alabama 35807

Glossary

Alpha Centauri: the nearest star system beyond our Sun. It is about 4.3 light-years away and is a triple system, meaning it is made up of three stars that rotate about each other.

astronomer: a person involved in the scientific study of the Universe and its various bodies.

atmosphere: the gases that surround a planet, star, or moon.

axis: the imaginary straight line about which a planet, star, or moon turns or spins.

billion: in North America — and in this book — the number represented by 1 followed by nine zeroes — 1,000,000,000. In some places, such as the United Kingdom (Britain), this number is called "a thousand million." In these places, one billion would then be represented by 1 followed by *12* zeroes — 1,000,000,000,000: a million million, a number known as a trillion in North America.

comet: an object made of ice, rock, and gas; has a vapor tail that may be seen when the comet's orbit brings it close to the Sun.

double planet: planets that circle each other.

eclipse: the partial or complete blocking of light from one astronomical body by another.

ellipse: an oval shape.

equator: the imaginary line around the middle of a planet that is always an equal distance from the two poles of the planet. The equator divides the planet into two half-spheres, or hemispheres.

gravity: the force that causes objects like the Earth and Moon to be attracted to one another.

methane gas: a colorless, odorless, flammable gas.

observatory: a building or other structure designed for watching and recording celestial objects or events.

Oort Cloud: a swarm of comets surrounding the Solar system, named after Jan Oort, the Dutch astronomer who suggested its existence in 1950.

orbit: the path that one celestial object follows as it circles, or revolves, around another.

pole: either end of the axis around which a planet, moon, or star rotates.

probe: a craft that travels in space, photographing celestial bodies and even landing on some of them.

satellite: a smaller body orbiting a larger body. The Moon is Earth's natural satellite. Sputnik 1 and 2 were Earth's first artificial satellites.

Solar system: the Sun with the planets and all other bodies, such as the asteroids, that orbit the Sun.

star: a mass of material, usually wholly gaseous, massive enough to initiate (or to have once initiated) nuclear reactions in its central regions.

Sun: our star and provider of the energy that makes life possible on Earth.

underworld: in Greek mythology, the place where it was believed people went when they died.

vaporize: to turn something that is liquid or solid into a gas.

wavelength: light, when viewed with certain instruments, makes a wavelike pattern. In any wave a wavelength is the distance from one maximum (peak) to the next.

Index

The publishers wish to thank the following for permission to reproduce copyright material: front cover, pp. 10, 17 (both), © Paul Dimare, 1989; p. 4, © Rick Karpinski/DeWalt and Associates, 1989; p. 5, copyright-free reproduction from Heck, J. G., *The Complete Encyclopedia of Illustration*; pp. 6, 12, © Keith Ward, 1989; p. 7 (all), Lowell Observatory photographs; pp. 8, 15 (upper two), © Lynette Cook, 1989; p. 9, © Julian Baum, 1989; p. 11, © Sally Bensusen, 1982; pp. 13 (upper), 15 (lower), 22, © Michael Carroll, 1989; pp. 13 (lower), 25, official US Navy photographs; p. 14, Kate Kriege, © Gareth Stevens, Inc., 1989; p. 14 (inset), courtesy of NASA; p. 16, © Stewart M. Green, Tom Stack and Associates; p. 18, © Joe Shabram, 1987; p. 19 (upper), Space Telescope Science Institute, courtesy of Marc W. Buie; p. 19 (lower), photograph by Matthew Groshek, © Gareth Stevens, Inc., 1989; pp. 20-21, © John Foster, 1985; p. 23 (all), Space Telescope Science Institute; p. 24 (both), Jet Propulsion Laboratory; p. 26, © Pat Rawlings, 1989; p. 27, © Michael Carroll; pp. 28-29, © Sally Bensusen, 1987; p. 29 (inset), © Sally Bensusen, 1989.